YAS

Face the Facts

Globalization

Adam Hibbert

For information, address the publisher:
Raintree, 100 N. LaSalle, Suite 1200, Chicago, IL 60602

Produced for Raintree by Monkey Puzzle Media Ltd.
Printed and bound in China by South China Printing Company.

09 08 07 06 05
10 9 8 7 6 5 4 3 2 1

Library of Congress Cataloging-in-Publication Data
Hibbert, Adam, 1968-
   Globalization / Adam Hibbert.
      p. cm. -- (Face the facts)
Includes bibliographical references and index.
Contents: What is globalization? -- Global economy -- Political links -- Global work -- Global culture -- Roots of globalization -- Modern history -- Technical development -- Economic development -- Globalization today -- Developing world -- Developed world -- Managing globalization -- International Monetary Fund -- World Bank -- World Trade Organization -- Civil society -- Why now? -- Fairness -- Democracy -- Security -- Environment -- Culture -- Globalization and you.
   ISBN 1-4109-1071-7 (cloth)
   1. International economic integration--Juvenile literature. 2. Globalization--Social aspects Juvenile literature. 3. Globalization--Economic aspects--Juvenile literature. 4. Globalization Environmental aspects--Juvenile literature. [1. Globalization. 2. Free trade. 3. International business enterprises. 4. International finance.] I. Title.
HF1418.5.H53 2004
337--dc22
2003025688

Acknowledgments
The publisher would like to thank the following for permission to reproduce copyright materials:
Alamy p. 16 (Robert Llewellyn/ImageState); Corbis pp. 24 (James A Sugar), 25 (Richard Berenholtz), 41 (Steve Raymer); DocumentChina p. 12 (Fritz Hoffmann); Eye Ubiquitous p. 7 (Paul Thompson); Fairtrade Foundation p. 49; Mark Henley pp. 4, 6, 21, 28, 29, 36, 46–47; Hulton Archive p. 14; Hutchison Library p. 23 top (Sarah Murray); Network Photographers pp. 11 (Andy Cleverley/Focus), 22–23 (Fritz Hoffmann), 27 (Jenny Matthews), 38 bottom (Christopher Pillitz), 43 (Jorg Wischmann), 44 (Nikolai Ignatief); PA Photos/EPA pp. 8, 9, 31; Panos Pictures pp. 18–19 (Trygve Bolstad), 34 (Caroline Penn), 37 (Andy Johnstone); Rex Features p. 38 top (Alex Segre); Topham Picturepoint p. 32–33 (Image Works). The artwork on p. 15 is by Michael Posen.

Cover photograph reproduced with permission of Panos Pictures (Dermot Tatlow).

Some words are shown in bold, **like this**. You can find out what they mean by looking in the glossary.

Contents

Introduction

Long before written history, human **societies** appeared in almost every region of the world—from the Inuit of the Arctic to the desert peoples of Africa and China. These societies were isolated (separate) from each other—contact between them was very rare. In the 21st century, that kind of isolation is almost impossible to imagine. The different societies of the world are now linked together in many ways—they are joining together as one global society. This process is called globalization.

Global economy

Today, products sold in stores in the United States, for example, often come from distant countries. When countries exchange goods in this way, they have **economic** links. As more and more of these economic links develop, the different economies of the world come together into one global economy.

Global politics

When countries were isolated from each other, each country's government could

"Globalization itself is neither good nor bad. It has the power to do enormous good—but for many, it seems closer to an unmitigated disaster."

Joseph Stiglitz, Nobel Prize winner for Economics

Entry by invitation only

decide on the rules for how their society should be run. Now that countries are linked in many ways, governments need to work together on some **political** issues. They create international political organizations to do this work. These bodies can make decisions that affect several countries.

Global work

More companies began to work globally (with offices and factories in several different countries) beginning in roughly 1980. Some companies have moved their jobs from one region to another, for example from Europe to Southeast Asia, where wages and other costs are lower. People from different countries may also move to wherever the jobs are.

Global culture

If one country is isolated from other countries, its **culture** is protected from change—it does not need to adapt to new or strange ideas. Globalization breaks down barriers between countries and affects local traditions. For example, through movies, television, and music, people around the world are being influenced by the culture of Western countries.

What this book does

The first section of this book examines these four aspects of globalization (economy, politics, work, and culture) in more detail. The book then explores the roots of globalization and examines how far the process has come today. It looks at what people are doing to try to manage globalization and explores political debates about whether they are successful. Finally, the book considers different ways in which people respond to the issues of globalization.

Globalization brings contrasting cultures together—a Western cola company delivers its drinks in Calcutta, India.

5

The Global Economy

Economic links are formed whenever goods and money are exchanged. These links can be simple, such as when a child spends his or her pocket money in a neighborhood store. They can also be more complex, involving the movement of large sums of money around the world. The global economy includes all economic links that involve goods or money moving from one country to another.

Global trade

Trade is the activity of making, buying, and selling goods. Each country has strengths and weaknesses when it comes to producing goods. For example, China is good at growing rice because it has a hot, wet climate. Saudi Arabia could not grow rice in its deserts but can produce oil. If China agrees to sell rice to Saudi Arabia in return for oil, both can focus on producing their best products. Benefits like this lead to the growth of global trade.

A rice farmer works her field by hand. China's large workforce and favorable climate make it a better place for growing rice than most other countries.

Currencies are bought and sold and complex investments are made at special markets called stock exchanges, such as this one in Tokyo, Japan.

Global loans

Banks and governments can help countries **develop** by lending them money. The debt is paid back, usually over a long period of time, with an additional payment called **interest**. Most loans are given by **developed countries** to **developing countries**. This can limit the choices available to politicians from developing countries—to obtain a loan, governments may have to agree to certain conditions. For example, they may have to agree to spend less on schools and hospitals so they can afford to pay back the money they borrow.

Global investment

People with large sums of money (capital) can save it in a bank. Their capital will grow a little because the bank will pay them a small amount of interest. But people with large amounts of capital usually find their money grows more quickly if they **invest** it—for example, they might buy part of a company and collect some of the company's **profits**.

Investments have become more global over the last 100 years. For example, an investor in France might try to predict that another country's **currency** (for example, the Singapore dollar) will gain value tomorrow compared to other currencies. The investor buys the dollars, then sells again once the value has risen. This kind of investment can cause large amounts of capital to pour into a country's economy—and out again—in just a few hours, as investors buy or sell the country's currency.

Global Politics

Politics is the act of running a country's government—deciding who should lead a **society** and how the society should be run. It involves making decisions about laws and how money from taxes should be spent. This can be difficult, even when it just involves the government and citizens of one country. Now that the countries of the world have closer ties, individual governments can no longer make all political decisions on their own. Some decisions need to be made at a global or international level, involving many countries working together.

For example, one country might want to introduce a law making it illegal to hunt and kill whales off its coasts. But whaling ships from other countries might be operating in the area, so all the countries involved need to work together if the ban on whaling is to succeed.

Global political campaigns

When people in different countries agree that a political change is needed, they can form an international political **campaign**. Cheaper air travel—and global communication links such as the Internet—have made this easier. The campaign can urge politicians in each country to work together to achieve the goal. The Jubilee campaign,

In Geneva, Switzerland, children from the Philippines, South Africa, and Brazil hold a banner for an international campaign against child labor.

for example, asks world leaders everywhere to cancel **debt payments** from the world's poorest countries to the richest ones.

represent poor farmers around the world. Instead of making political decisions at the national level, these groups make politics international.

Groups of countries

Different countries in regions around the world sometimes form groups that work together to make political decisions. For example, many of the nations in Europe have joined the European Union (EU) and work together on many issues. Countries in other regions of the world, such as the Middle East and Southeast Asia, have also formed regional groups. In 2003, China, India, and Brazil created a new group of 21 countries to

Global bodies

Since the early 20th century, countries around the world have tried to find ways to work together and cooperate with each other. They created the **United Nations** (UN) in 1945. The UN is not a world government, but countries send representatives to meetings of the UN to discuss and vote on global political issues such as international peace and security.

At the United Nations, countries vote on important issues, such as this vote which was about helping to rebuild Iraq after the war in 2003.

Global Work

People often leave their home town, or even country, to find work where more jobs are available. In China, for example, more than 60 million peasants have moved from poor rural areas to look for work in the rapidly growing cities along the coast. With cheaper international travel, more **migration** from poor regions to richer ones is expected. Migration raises strong emotions, especially for poor people within rich countries, who worry that people arriving from other countries will compete with them for jobs.

The price of a person

Some countries can afford to care for people who cannot find a job. Governments pay them money (welfare) to support them while they are jobless. Welfare is expensive. The money comes from taxes, which are paid to the government by businesses and by individuals. In poorer countries that cannot afford a welfare system, poverty forces people to accept very low-paying jobs, or to rely on their children or parents to help them earn a living.

Migrating jobs

Companies can move their place of business to employ people in poorer countries, where they can pay people less than in their own countries. So, while people sometimes move from poorer countries to richer ones to find work, some jobs migrate from richer countries to poorer ones. This may leave some people in richer countries unemployed and dependent on welfare.

Case study Telecommuting in India

Now that businesses use global communication links (including telephones and computers) for many jobs, there is no reason why these jobs have to be done by people in one particular country. Many well-educated people in India are employed in telecommuting—this means they work for companies based in other countries, using telephone and computer links. For example, the computer system that controls the water supply in London is managed by a team in Hyderabad, India. Indian workers also work in call centers (offices that handle telephone inquiries), for distant companies. English-speaking Indian employees deal with customer inquiries from all over the world. By 2003, India employed over 100,000 workers in such jobs, up from 26,000 in 2001. The wages paid to people who work in these jobs in India are much lower than in **developed countries**.

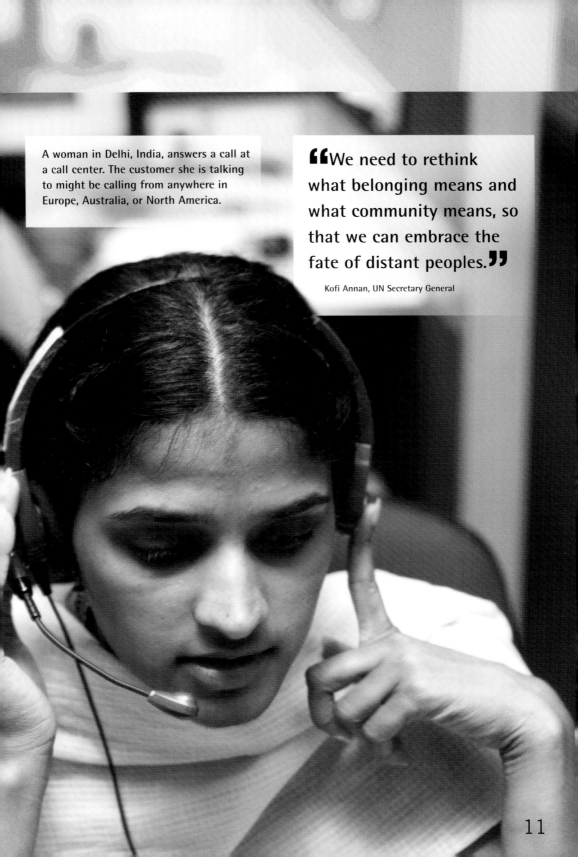

A woman in Delhi, India, answers a call at a call center. The customer she is talking to might be calling from anywhere in Europe, Australia, or North America.

"We need to rethink what belonging means and what community means, so that we can embrace the fate of distant peoples."

Kofi Annan, UN Secretary General

Global Culture

All of the world's **cultures** are influenced by globalization. As goods and **services** are exchanged between different countries, the cultures of those countries are also affected. For example, movies, TV shows, and advertisements from the United States are seen all over the world and have influenced the way of life in many countries. The cultures of poor countries can also influence wealthier ones. For example, pop music in rich **Western** countries, is strongly influenced by African culture—jazz, the blues, and Afro-Jamaican reggae music styles. Salsa dancing, which originated in Latin American countries, is becoming increasingly popular in countries such as the United Kingdom, along with contemporary African and traditional world music.

Cultural goods

Many aspects of cultural life in **developed countries** are linked to the buying and selling of goods. For example, in the West, music, art, literature, fashion, and food are closely tied to the buying and selling of goods—CDs, works of art, books, clothes, and brands of food. These cultural goods can be moved around the world and sold to other countries, where they might influence other cultures.

In poorer **societies**, cultural activities are not as connected with the buying and selling of goods. They are often part of the daily life and traditions of a community, in which everyone joins in with the activity, such as dancing or playing music. This kind of cultural activity cannot be bought or sold, or easily moved from one community to another. In some cases, wealthy tourists will pay to come and watch these activities. But as traditional lifestyles change, these cultural practices can be lost.

Global language

The power of the British economy in the 19th century and the U.S. economy in the 20th century has made English a useful language for business people. It is the main language on the Internet and up to a quarter of the world's population can speak some English. Many find this unfair, particularly because English can be so difficult to learn. As global languages such as English take over, between 3,000 and 4,000 local languages are expected to die out.

Melting pots

Globalization can be a threat to cultures that are shared only by small groups of people. But it can also lead groups of people to settle in new places, bringing aspects of their culture to new countries. In this way, cultures blend together in a melting pot of global influences, especially in cities with large **immigrant** populations.

Many Chinese children, like these seen here playing a video game, now share the same culture with children all around the world.

Trading Links

China, the Middle East, northern and eastern Africa, and Europe have been connected by **trade** routes for thousands of years. Greek, Roman, Arabic, and Mongol **empires** created strong trade links between these regions. In roughly 1450 C.E., Europeans began to explore beyond these regions, gradually bringing central and southern Africa, Australia, and the Americas into one global network of trade.

European empires

The years from 1450 to the 20th century were an age of European empires. European countries competed to control trade with distant **societies**, forming empires that linked the globe as never before. For example, Portugal took control of parts of West and East Africa, Spain conquered parts of South America, Britain and France fought for control of North America, and Britain and Holland struggled over Southeast Asia and southern Africa.

New industries

The **Industrial Revolution** in European countries led to even more trade in the late 18th and 19th centuries. The trade in jute, a plant fiber used to make rope and burlap bags, is a good example of the way new trade links developed. With the invention of new machines in Britain, jute grown in India was shipped all the way to Britain to be processed. Jute rope and burlap bags were shipped back to India for sale. Despite the cost of shipping, the machine-made goods still cost less than similar goods handmade locally.

Global chill

Global trade increased in the 20th century, but not without interruption. During World War I (1914–18) and World War II (1939–45) and in the period between the wars, most countries tried to protect themselves from unemployment and other **economic** disasters by cutting off trade links with

This drawing shows Dutch traders and Native Americans in approximately 1750. The traders are buying valuable furs to sell in Europe.

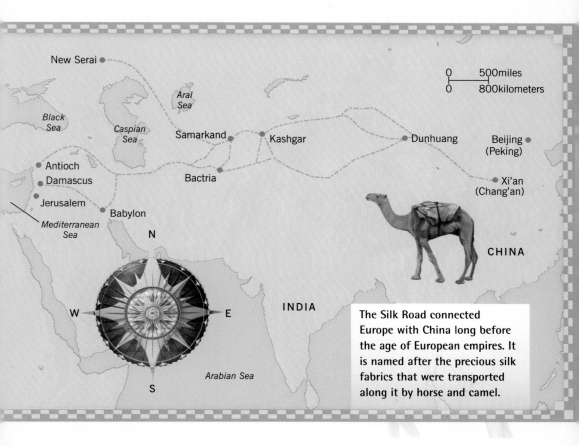

New Serai

Aral
Sea

Black
Sea

Caspian
Sea

Samarkand

Kashgar

Dunhuang

Beijing
(Peking)

Antioch

Damascus

Bactria

Xi'an
(Chang'an)

Jerusalem

Babylon

Mediterranean
Sea

N

CHINA

W

E

INDIA

Arabian Sea

S

0   500miles
0   800kilometers

The Silk Road connected
Europe with China long before
the age of European empires. It
is named after the precious silk
fabrics that were transported
along it by horse and camel.

each other. They believed their own companies would be protected if people stopped buying goods from foreign companies. Trade was also affected during the Cold War (1945–90). This was a period of hostility between nations that were at that time **communist** (such as the **USSR** and countries in Eastern Europe) and **democratic** nations (such as the United States and countries in Western Europe).

1980s and beyond

In the 1980s, global trading grew sharply as **Western** companies tried to find new opportunities in other countries. By 1990, most large businesses were working globally (making and selling goods in many different countries). Globalization sped up again during the 1990s—from 1991 to 1996, the value of goods being exchanged between countries grew at seven percent each year.

Globalization and Technical Progress

The history of globalization goes hand in hand with new inventions. In the 1400s and 1500s, a simple new map or navigation tool could help a ship arrive at its destination more quickly and safely. In the 21st century, we can save ships from storms by monitoring the sea from space, using satellites. Making global connections more efficient reaps big rewards, so a lot of research goes into it.

Global communications

Until the 1830s, the fastest way to send a message long-distance was to strap it to the leg of a carrier pigeon. In 1837, the first telegraph systems were invented, allowing messages to be sent from one place to another along a wire. A cable linking the United States to Europe was laid under the sea in 1866. Telephone networks, radio, television, fax machines, satellite communications, computers, mobile phones, and the Internet all followed within 130 years.

These technologies allow people to interact wherever they are around the world. For example, scientists around the world use the Internet to share discoveries and work together, speeding up scientific progress.

People no longer have to travel to talk to each other face-to-face. Internet connections let people hold conversations through video conferences from opposite sides of the world.

Air transportation

When people are working together as a team, they may need to meet and talk face-to-face. But travel over land tends to be slow, and travel by sea is even slower. The development of air travel has made it possible to reach the other side of the globe in less than a day, so teams can have members all around the world.

Air transportation also allows short-lived goods, such as fresh flowers, to be grown in one country and sold in another within a few hours before they spoil. In 1950, almost all imports to the United States arrived by boat. By 2000, one third of imports arrived on planes.

Super ships

Many types of bulky items are transported around the world by **cargo** ships. It became easier to transport goods by ship in the 1960s, when shippers in different countries agreed to use a standard-sized box (called a container) for cargo. Cranes lift containers on and off semi trucks, trains, and ships, with as little handling time as possible, making it more efficient to move goods around the world.

Global Competition

The growth of global **trade** has important effects on the **economies** of individual countries. World trade has allowed **Western** countries to increase their wealth by selling inexpensive, manufactured goods to countries that are less **developed**. World trade has also given **developing countries** a chance to sell their products to wealthy Western **consumers**, helping some of them increase their wealth. As a result, the economies of some countries in Southeast Asia, such as South Korea and Taiwan, have grown rapidly during the past 25 years, with companies making everything from food to cars and computers.

World trade and competition

When businesses can sell their goods without having to compete with foreign rivals, it can make them inefficient. They do not have to use the best methods or supply goods as cheaply as possible. Global **competition** forces companies to stay up-to-date—if they fall behind, a company from another country can win over their customers.

Unemployment

Companies that lose out to competition from abroad are sometimes driven out of business. This causes unemployment and other problems. In Western countries, the unemployed normally receive welfare and retraining for new jobs. The effects of unemployment can be more life-threatening in poor countries.

Many of Europe's fresh flowers come from Kenya. Kenya can compete with European flower growers because of fast air-delivery links and low labor costs.

Case study
'Just-in-time' at Toyota

The competition between the Japanese car manufacturer Toyota and the U.S. company General Motors is a good example of global rivals. When they buy parts to make their cars, manufacturers normally borrow money for the parts from a bank. Every day, they have to pay **interest** on the money they have borrowed. This extra cost is added to the cost of making the cars, making each car a bit more expensive to buy.

To cut these costs, Toyota runs a 'just-in-time' policy. It buys car parts 'just-in-time' to build each car. The parts are supplied by businesses located up to only 60 miles (100 kilometers) away who can deliver car parts up to eight times a day. General Motors buys its parts from suppliers who are often much further away—an average 420 miles (680 kilometers). This means Toyota has to borrow money from the bank for less time—so it pays less interest. Because Toyota's costs are smaller than those of General Motors it can sell very similar cars at a slightly lower price.

Measuring Globalization

The speed at which the world's **economy** and **cultures** are joining together has increased over the last 30 years. Increased **trade** links with other countries have helped **Western** economies become stronger. International trade has also strengthened the economies of some **developing countries**. As wealth has increased, the quality of life has improved in many poor places. But while globalization has helped some countries, many of the world's poorest countries, such as those in Africa, still have high levels of poverty and very weak economies.

Measuring the global economy

How do we know that globalization has increased? There are some economic indicators that help us get a clear picture. The simplest measure is to add up all the money spent in a year by people trading things with people in other countries. According to this measure, global trade is twenty times bigger than it was in 1950 (see page 50 for details).

Another measure is Gross Domestic Product (GDP). GDP is the total value of everything (all goods and **services**) produced in a country in any year. By adding together the GDPs of every country, we can see that the world's GDP was six times bigger in 2000 than in 1950.

These two sets of numbers can be analyzed. This lets us see whether trade between countries has become a more important part of the world economy, or whether it has just grown in the same way as other aspects of the world economy. By this count, global trade is three times more important in our daily lives than it was in 1950 (see page 50).

Other measures

There are other examples, rather than just the world's economy, we can use to study aspects of globalization. The number of people **migrating** from one country to another is one example. This measure shows a strange trend in globalization—while more goods and services are moving between countries, people appear to be migrating less than they were 100 years ago (see page 51 for details). It is hard to measure the more cultural aspects of globalization. However, in 1999, a **UN** survey found that more than three-quarters of all World Wide Web material was written in English. A 2002 study found that the number had dropped to an estimated one-half.

Measuring attitudes

Very few studies have been carried out to compare attitudes to globalization in different regions of the world. The PEW Global Attitudes Project was a survey of 38,000 people across 44 countries. It found that people in developing countries are more positive about the benefits of global trade than people in wealthy countries.

High-tech cargo ports, like this one in Hong Kong, are vital for handling goods traded between countries.

The Developing World

Poorer countries are often called **developing countries**. These countries have not **developed** their economies (increased their wealth) to the level of the world's richest places, such as North America, Europe, or Japan. The poorest countries of the world are in Africa, Central and South America, and Asia.

Global trade and development success

Taken as a whole, developing countries have a greater share of world **trade** today than at any time in the past. In 1971, 19 percent of all goods and **services** traded in the world were from developing countries. In 2000, the figure had risen to 32 percent.

An estimated ten developing countries, mainly in Asia, have enjoyed large economic **growth** since 1980—they have increased their wealth, improved standards of living, and reduced poverty. They have been able to do this because they have become more open to world trade.

The world's poorest countries

While some countries have benefited from global trade, the poorest 49 countries, with roughly 500 million people, share less than one percent of world trade. Some have even suffered a decrease in their standard of living. In Africa, for example, almost half of all people live in poverty, while one in three children under the age of five suffers from **malnutrition**. The world's poorest countries struggle to make **debt payments** to richer countries, and some have to deal with the effects of civil wars.

The world's poorest countries often sell a small range of simple products, such as coffee beans. The price of many of these goods has fallen in recent years, so farmers have to sell their products to wealthy countries at very low prices. The benefits of trading are lost, and small farmers are forced out of work.

Benin, Africa, needs to sell unprocessed cotton to earn money from abroad. African countries risk poverty when international prices drop for goods like this.

Development success in China

Between 1978 and 1994, China's **economy** grew by 9 percent each year. The value of goods it sold to other countries grew by 14 percent each year and it earned more money from selling goods to other countries than it spent on buying goods from other countries (see page 51 for details). Living standards improved and people began to earn more money. In 2000, working people in China earned roughly three times more than they did in 1980. In the United States during the same period wages rose by half.

China's developing economy needs thousands of new offices, factories, and homes.

The Developed World

Wealthy nations with high standards of living are described as **developed countries**—these include the United States, Japan, Australia, New Zealand, and the countries of Europe. A developed country has many different businesses, a reliable system of laws and government, a well-built network of roads and railways, schools, and well-equipped hospitals for everybody.

Developed countries are in the best position to benefit from the growth in global **trade** links. Their businesses use the latest technology to create goods cheaply. But globalization affects different members of these **societies** in different ways.

Changing cultures

Globalization has had an effect on the **cultures** of developed countries, especially in cities that have large **immigrant** communities. When immigrant communities settle in developed countries, they bring with them some of their own cultural traditions. They also help increase trade links between their new home and their country of origin.

For example, as Chinese and Indian people have **migrated** to **Western** cities, they have shared their tastes for traditional Asian foods with local people. Demand for these foods has grown in Western countries, and more of these foods are now being **imported** from Asia.

Changing economies

Some manufacturing companies are moving their factories from Western countries to cheaper places, in Asia and other developing regions, where they can pay workers lower wages than in the West. This may cut the number of

U.S. beef farming (like this beef farm in California) is very efficient, but still needs support from the government to survive—support some countries think is unfair.

manufacturing jobs available to people in wealthy countries. They are more likely to find work in **service** industries, such as shop work or cleaning, which cannot be done from a distance.

Farming in developed countries

Governments in developed countries give support in the form of **subsidies** (money) to their farmers. Farmers in the United States, European Union countries, and Japan together receive an estimated $300 billion each year from their governments. One study has found that every cow in the United States receives $2.90 per day from the government—a higher income than half of the world's working people earn.

Because farmers in developed countries receive subsidies from their governments, they can sell their produce cheaply all over the world. It is difficult for farmers from poor countries, who do not receive extra money from their governments, to compete.

Cities such as New York thrive on a mixture of cultures. As manufacturing jobs move abroad, these cities are turning to service industries such as tourism.

The UN and Other Rule Makers

When World War II ended in 1945, an international organization called the **United Nations (UN)** was created to stop international arguments from leading to another war. Governments hoped that the UN could agree on fair codes of conduct (rules of behavior) so countries could work out their differences without violence. The UN now has 191 member countries and its headquarters are in New York. Its work includes international peacekeeping, assisting countries with **economic** and social **development**, and protecting **human rights**.

There are three special international organizations that handle global economic issues. These are the **International Monetary Fund (IMF)**, the **World Bank**, and the **World Trade Organization (WTO)**.

The IMF

During the 1920s and 1930s, **Western** countries such as the United States and Germany experienced crises in their economies, with high **inflation** and millions of people out of work. In 1944, a fund of money was created to protect countries from such crises in the future—the IMF.

The World Bank

World War II destroyed many basic facilities in many countries—railways, roads, ports, power systems, water supplies, and so on. At the end of the war, a new bank was set up to lend money to these countries so they could repair the damage. This was the International Bank for Reconstruction and Development (IBRD), which became known as the World Bank.

This school in Rwanda, Africa, does not even have a solid floor.

UNESCO - P
UNICEF - RU
T.E.P

The World Trade Organization (WTO)

Between the two world wars, **developed countries** limited **trade** with each other in an attempt to protect their own businesses and jobs. Since 1945, people have argued that global trade should be freed of these restraints to encourage **economic growth**—this is known as the **free trade** argument. The World Trade Organization (WTO) was founded in 1995 to help to remove barriers to free trade.

International rules

Sometimes a country's government or voters disagree with the rules created by these bodies. It is up to that country to decide whether it will follow the rules or risk being punished. If a country breaks international rules, the UN may decide to exclude it from international meetings or from trade with other countries. In extreme cases the UN can even threaten military action against the rule-breaker.

Globalization and the IMF

The **International Monetary Fund (IMF)** tries to help countries manage their **currencies**. It does this by giving advance warning of problems, advising governments about their **economies**, and lending large sums of money to countries in times of crisis.

The IMF is based in Washington, D.C. It is governed by its 184 member countries. Each member pays money to the fund. The amount each member pays determines how much say it has in IMF decisions. The United States contributes over seventeen percent and has seventeen percent of the votes. China contributes roughly three percent of the fund's money, and controls roughly three percent of the votes.

Culture trouble?

Some people argue that the IMF does not benefit all countries equally. Different countries have different **cultures** and styles of economy, but the IMF's rules, which are made by **Western** economists (experts in economics), often ignore these differences. In Asia there are now plans to develop a local alternative to the IMF that reflects local culture better.

Jakarta, the capital of Indonesia, is shown here. Under the IMF's economic rules, life became much tougher for some Indonesians and there were widespread protests and riots in 1998.

"There are about ten universities in the United States and the United Kingdom that supply the overwhelming majority of the [IMF] staff."

Professor Martha Finnemore, George Washington University, Washington, D.C.

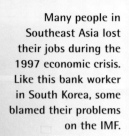

Many people in Southeast Asia lost their jobs during the 1997 economic crisis. Like this bank worker in South Korea, some blamed their problems on the IMF.

Case study The IMF and Asia

On July 2, 1997, the national currency of Thailand, the Baht, fell in value—that is, its value dropped compared to the currencies of other countries. Previously, one Baht had been equal to roughly four U.S. cents, but its value fell to roughly three cents. This caused serious problems for Thailand's economy. It looked as if the crisis would spread to other Asian countries.

To control the problem, Thailand, Indonesia, South Korea, and other countries asked the IMF to lend them money. They used the extra money to strengthen their economies. As part of the deal, these countries agreed to change how they ran their economies, following rules set down by the IMF.

Some people believe that the IMF work on this crisis was a great success. The crisis did not spread across the world, and Asian economies became stable again rather quickly. Other people argue that it was a disaster. They say the IMF placed unfair economic rules on the countries that took its loans, making life much harder than necessary for poor people in the region. Two countries that rejected IMF advice—Malaysia and China—survived the crisis fairly well.

Globalization and the World Bank

When the **World Bank** was first set up in 1944, near the end of World War II, it was designed to lend money to countries so they could repair damage caused during the war. It now lends money to poor countries with the goal of helping them **develop** (increase their wealth). There are 184 member countries that contribute money and decide how the money should be used. Its headquarters are in Washington, D.C. The World Bank makes roughly $20 billion available each year to the world's 100 poorest countries.

World Bank loans and grants

The World Bank offers different types of help to **developing countries**. In 2003, it gave out $11 billion in **grants** and **interest-free credit**. The World Bank also gives low-**interest** loans—money that has to be paid back plus an extra charge (interest) on top of the amount borrowed.

The difference it makes

It is difficult to measure the effect of the World Bank's many loans and projects. The Bank believes that it has helped to rescue millions of the world's poorest people from poverty, improving their access to jobs, health **services**, and education. But it also admits, for example, that roughly three out of four of its projects in Africa fail.

The World Bank says that the main reason so many of its projects fail is that governments misuse the money. Some loans for development projects have been stopped because, rather than being used on the intended project, money from the World Bank has disappeared into the pockets of government officials or the companies that work for them. This leaves a few people very rich, while the country and its people have to pay back the debt.

Debt payments

The poorest countries in the world are now repaying the money they have borrowed in the past. Poor countries spend more money each year repaying their debts to rich countries than rich countries spend on helping poor countries develop. Some people argue that the **debt payments** made by poor countries have to be stopped to allow poor countries to escape poverty. The World Bank is one of the best sources for countries to make agreements to end the debt.

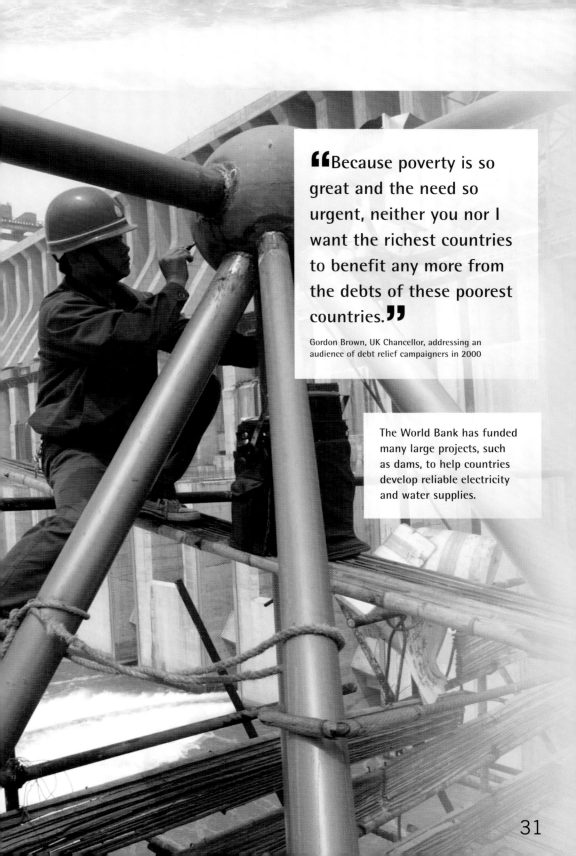

"Because poverty is so great and the need so urgent, neither you nor I want the richest countries to benefit any more from the debts of these poorest countries."

Gordon Brown, UK Chancellor, addressing an audience of debt relief campaigners in 2000

The World Bank has funded many large projects, such as dams, to help countries develop reliable electricity and water supplies.

Globalization and the WTO

The **World Trade Organization (WTO)** was set up in 1995. Its headquarters are in Geneva, Switzerland. With 146 member countries, it has a role in 97 percent of world **trade**, and most of the other countries in the world have applied for membership. The WTO was set up to monitor **free trade** between countries, to settle trade disputes, and to oversee the setting up of new trade agreements between countries.

Free trade

WTO members accept certain rules. In particular, they agree to trade freely. This means they are not supposed to put barriers in the way of trade links between countries, such as by charging taxes on goods that are **imported** into their country. In return, they benefit from being allowed to sell their goods without barriers to customers in other member countries.

Tariffs

Tariffs are a type of tax placed on goods when they are imported into a country. The WTO works to reduce tariffs because it believes they get in the way of free trade. Tariffs make imported goods seem more expensive and may discourage imports of those goods. Tariffs can also be complex to work with, so they may hinder trade by making it difficult and costly.

Unpopular

The WTO has become the main target of anti-globalization **campaigns**. Campaigners say that poor countries are bullied at WTO meetings into accepting new trade rules that only benefit **Western** businesses. The WTO contends that it offers poor countries their best opportunity to work together and have a voice in decisions about world trade.

China's example

In 2001, China was accepted into the WTO. Within six months, China had changed 2,300 laws and dropped another 830 laws to meet WTO rules on free trade. In 2002, China's **exports** (goods sold to other countries) in one industry alone—farm produce—grew by 13.3 percent. Benefits such as this encourage other **developing countries** to join the WTO.

The HTS

Goods entering the United States are classed according to a detailed list, called the Harmonized Tariff Schedule (HTS). The printed HTS is a large document, eight inches (twenty centimeters) thick. Different items are charged a tariff at different rates, which can change each year. This can make it difficult for traders to know how much tax they will have to pay on goods they ship into the United States, so it can be difficult for them to know if it will be worthwhile. Tariff changes can turn a good deal into a costly mistake. Most wealthy countries have similar systems.

This massive protest took place in 1999 during a WTO conference in Seattle. This began a new trend for protests against globalization.

❝ In a way, the WTO is the UN for trade. ❞

Pascal Lamy, Trade Commissioner for the EU

Global Communities

While governments try to manage the global **economy** through the **IMF**, **WTO**, and **World Bank**, other groups of people try to influence global **society** through Non-Governmental Organizations (NGOs). These are organizations that are not controlled by any of the world's governments. Some focus on helping companies in different countries work together. Some encourage understanding and friendship between people from different **cultures**. Others try to bring support to poorer people around the world through education, healthcare, and other programs.

Trade associations

Companies form international clubs, called **trade** associations, to share ideas about what their industry needs and how it will develop. For example, the International Iron and Steel Institute (IISI) brings steel producers from around the world together to share information and determine how to help their industry

achieve success. Associations such as the IISI help people around the world work together.

Charities

Charities are organizations that are funded by gifts, either from individuals or from companies. Many charities deal with problems caused by poverty all around the world. For example, charities work to deliver food to starving people and to bring

Money donated by a charity is used to pay for a new water supply in Hitosa, Ethiopia. Villagers work alongside the experts.

healthcare to countries that do not have proper health **services**. They are also involved in providing care and legal help to **immigrants** and **refugees**.

Belief groups

Some groups try to bring people from different cultures together peacefully by promoting shared beliefs and values. Religious organizations usually promote one set of religious beliefs— Christianity or Islam, for example. They may provide schools or support for the poor, inspiring others to join their community.

There are similar groups that are not religious. For example, the International Humanist and Ethical Union (IHEU) was founded in 1952 to promote **human rights** and friendship between all humans, without promoting religion.

Internet communities

The Internet enables people from many cultures to communicate and exchange ideas. This creates communities of ordinary people who are able to share news from around the world. These communities promote shared global experiences instead of local or national ones.

The Globalization Debate

Globalization is a hot topic in **politics**. Tens of thousands of people gather to protest against globalization whenever the **WTO** has a conference. Other people try to defend globalization as a positive influence on our world. Governments have to try to find a balance—on the one hand they need to have some control over what happens in their country's **economy**, but on the other hand they want to benefit from global **trade**, which is out of their control.

Why now?

Some experts are puzzled by what a hot topic globalization is. It has been happening for hundreds of years, they argue, so why are people suddenly interested in it? People on this side of the globalization debate are called skeptics—they doubt that the idea really means anything. Skeptics are usually neither for nor against globalization. Instead, they try to look behind the issue to see why people are moved by it.

New community?

Some people believe that nations must act together over issues such as the environment, climate change, or global **human rights**. They believe that it is no longer acceptable for nations to do their own thing, and argue that globalization is a good thing since it encourages countries to act as a global community and accept global codes of conduct.

New empire?

Some people oppose globalization and agree with the skeptics that it is not a new process. They argue that the dream of a friendly, global **society** is just an excuse for rich, **Western** countries to form a new type of **empire**. According to

These protesters against globalization believe that human needs should take priority over the needs of the economy.

this view, the wealthy countries are making slaves out of poor countries. Instead of invading and conquering as they did in the past, they are using the threat of economic isolation to make poor countries obey them.

Anti-capitalist

The economies of Western countries are often called **capitalist** economies—this means that the trade and industry in these countries are controlled by businesses whose goal is to make a **profit**. Some people feel strongly that it is wrong that so many aspects of their lives are affected by the need for companies to make a profit through buying and selling things. This side of the debate can be described as anti-capitalist. Anti-globalization protesters often use the slogan "Our World Is Not For Sale," arguing that human needs should take priority over business success.

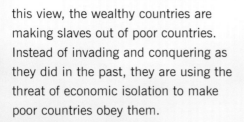

The arrival of the oil industry in Sumgayit, Azerbaijan, means big changes for the local people and for the environment. Are changes like this more significant today than in the past?

Is Globalization Fair?

Most anti-globalization **campaigners** believe that globalization is unfair. They say that it is not good for everyone—it works to the advantage of the rich countries and against the poorest people in **developing countries**. Many global **trade** links were established as European **empires** expanded in the 18th and 19th centuries. Unfairness was common at that time. Are modern global links any more fair?

A level playing field?

The rules governing global trade may appear the same for everyone, but there are two important reasons why the truth may be more complicated. First, when **Western** countries were **developing** their **economies** they often set restrictions on trade. For example, the United Kingdom sometimes limited corn **imports** to protect its farmers from having to compete with cheaper corn from other countries. Some people believe that protections of this kind may be a necessary part of a developing economy, even today. Second, wealthy countries can use their power to avoid having to stick to the rules, while weaker countries have to obey the rules strictly—or risk being excluded from trade with other countries.

These consumers drink coffee in a London cafe. A small share of the money they spend goes to Kenya to pay coffee farmers.

These Kenyan coffee farm workers have long days, doing boring, heavy work. They get paid very little money compared to the wages in the West.

Rich and poor

Anti-globalization campaigners argue that even when a developing country's economy grows because of increased trade with other countries, this often benefits just a few powerful people in the country, at the expense of the country's poorest people.

The gap between the income of the richest and poorest countries has been growing. In 1973, the richest countries were thirteen times richer than the poorest countries. By the year 2000 the richest were nineteen times richer than the poorest. This has been explained in different ways by those in favor of globalization and those against it.

Supporters of globalization point to the rapid **economic growth** in China and steady growth in India. These countries appear to prove that global trading helps fight poverty. Opponents of globalization point out that India and China both used **trade controls** to help their economies grow. They argue that other causes, such as debts to Western countries, are keeping the poorest countries poor.

> ❝ We are ready to be exploited, but we must be fairly exploited. ❞
>
> Mahathir Mohamad, former Prime Minister of Malaysia, October 2003

39

Globalization and Democracy

In a **democracy**, people elect politicians to represent them in government. This gives them a voice in how their country is run. But when countries take part in global **trade**, they have to accept certain international rules—such as how to tax and spend money. The global rules, nicknamed the Golden Straitjacket, may not be what the voters of a nation would want if they were free to choose.

Who rules—voters or business?

Large companies now operate globally, with workers in many different countries. These companies are known as multinationals. To compete with each other, they need to keep their costs low. So they often choose to operate in countries that offer low costs—for example, where taxes or wages are low. But what if voters in those countries want their governments to increase minimum wage levels, or increase taxes so there is more money to spend on schools and hospitals? That would raise costs, which could lead to companies moving their business to another country. For some people, this seems like blackmail—"Do not vote that way, or we take our business to another country."

Global votes

There is a serious debate over whether globalization is bad for democracy— governments face a tough choice between what voters want and what the global **economy** will allow. One answer would be to make sure that the bodies that manage global trade—such as the **WTO**—fairly represent all the world's citizens and only make rules that a majority of the world's population supports.

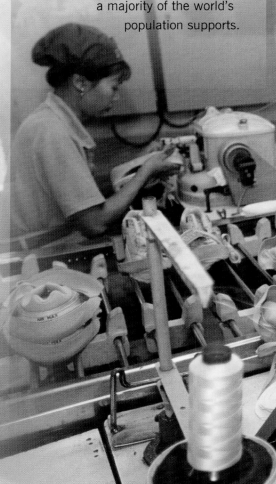

Most people think this is unlikely to happen. If WTO decisions were based on the number of voters in each country, the wealthy nations (with a total of roughly one billion people) would have to accept decisions made by the less wealthy ones (with a total of roughly five billion people). A second problem is that poor countries often cannot afford to take part in international decisions. As many as 30 **developing countries** have no office in Geneva, where WTO activities regularly take place.

Benefits

There are some reasons to argue that globalization may benefit democracy. The promise of **economic development** could encourage nations to improve their record on **human rights**. This is because countries that do not obey international rules on human rights may be excluded from global trade.

Roughly 50,000 Vietnamese workers have well-paid jobs making footwear for one Western employer. Vietnam won this business after agreeing to accept some international rules.

Global Security

The **UN**, the **IMF**, the **World Bank**, and the **WTO** were all set up in the hope that countries could peacefully work together for better living standards. World **trade** was seen as a way to bring people together in one global society, which would be more secure against conflict. When two countries depend on each other for their food supply, for example, a war between them is much less likely to start. But conflict still exists and the movement of people and goods between countries is seen as a new threat to security.

Poverty and insecurity

Improved living standards help societies to enjoy peace and social harmony. In the poorest regions of the world, where people have to fight for survival every day, security often breaks down. The causes of the civil wars that harmed Africa in the 1990s are complex, but poverty was an important issue. When **developing countries** increase their wealth and improve standards of living for their people, security usually improves.

Global police

An international organization for police work, Interpol, began work in 1946,

Specially trained dogs can sniff out bombs and other weapons in luggage, but dogs cannot search all of the goods passing through busy ports.

with its headquarters in France. Countries eventually joined the organization and it now has 181 members. Countries have used Interpol to help each other catch criminals or terrorists who could otherwise move from one country to another to escape the law.

Global terror

Some people around the world belong to religious or **political** groups that have given up hope of achieving change through politics and have chosen to act

through terrorism instead. In total, though, the number of acts of international terrorism fell from as many as 665 in 1987 to 190 in 2003, according to the U.S. State Department.

Trade and security

The terror attack in the United States on September 11, 2001, which killed over 3,000 people, used hijacked passenger planes as flying bombs to crash into buildings in New York City and Washington, D.C. Since the attack, air travel has become more heavily policed, and strict checks are now carried out on passengers and their baggage. But wealthy nations are too dependent on trade to stop goods coming in from abroad, and there are too many goods entering these countries for all packages to be searched as they arrive from overseas. New security measures were created for air **cargo** in the United States in November 2003, with random searches of packages. The extra costs and time delays caused by this new security work have to be paid by airlines and their customers.

Globalization and the Environment

Over the last 40 years, concern for the environment has grown stronger. Many environmental issues affect the whole world, and all nations need to act together if they want to protect the environment.

It is difficult to get different countries to agree on what should be done to protect the environment, since these decisions require countries to accept costs that will harm their **economic growth**. Even when it seems to be in everyone's interests to protect the environment, introducing environmental rules will usually cost some countries more than others.

Kyoto Protocol

In practice, it has been very difficult for countries to reach environmental agreements. The Kyoto Protocol—a list of promises drawn up at a conference in 1997—was meant to help prevent **global warming**. But not all of the world's **developed countries** agreed with or kept these promises. The Kyoto Protocol would force them to pay for expensive alternatives to polluting fossil fuels (oil, coal, and gas).

The United States suggested alternatives to the agreement, while the European Union members signed it. Despite signing, EU emissions of greenhouse gases (gases that may add to global warming) continued to rise in the 21st century. Countries in the European Union have found it difficult to make the necessary changes without causing **economic** problems.

Hidden agenda?

In 2001, the **WTO** brought leaders from 142 countries together at Doha, in Qatar, to discuss which issues they wanted to deal with in a new round of **trade** talks. The environment was a big issue. Some wealthy countries want to be able to control **imports** of goods when they suspect their production may have harmed the environment—for example, crops grown using **pesticides** banned in the West.

But many poor countries say that these environmental trade controls have a hidden purpose: Rich countries can use them to protect their industries—especially farming—from fair **competition** from other countries. Blocking imports in this way means **Western** farmers can charge higher prices for their own products because they do not have to compete with cheaper products from other countries.

The U.S. Clean Air Act and U.S. Endangered Species Act are two laws enacted by the United States to protect the environment. However, both have been condemned by the WTO, which believes these laws exclude **developing countries** from selling produce. The Clean Air Act blocked Venezuelan oil from sale in the United States, while the Endangered Species Act affected importers of shrimp.

❝The Kyoto Protocol will do nothing measurable about global warming and would cost this country [unfairly]. It's that simple.❞

Patrick Michaels, Cato Institute (a public policy research foundation), Washington, D.C.

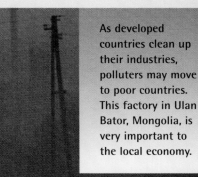

As developed countries clean up their industries, polluters may move to poor countries. This factory in Ulan Bator, Mongolia, is very important to the local economy.

Globalization and Culture

In more **developed countries**, where people do not have to worry about problems of daily survival, globalization may still seem threatening because of the changes it can bring to local **culture**.

Globalization and language

The U.S. leadership of the world **economy** has caused the English language to become more important around the world. European citizens see so many U.S. cultural products—such as television shows—that some English words fall into daily use in their languages. In some countries, such as France, the government sometimes tries to eliminate the English influence, usually without success. But governments can support local language and culture in other ways. For example, they can encourage filmmakers to use their local language by eliminating some of the tax costs other businesses have to pay.

Local industry

Industries associated with local culture are among the few that cannot be moved abroad. People working in jobs that have a strong cultural side— design, advertising, fashion, television, movies, art, music, food, and so on— cannot be replaced by people from other regions of the world. To succeed in these jobs, workers need local knowledge and experience of being part of that culture. Some people argue that, as other jobs relocate, these local culture industries will become a more important part of the economy—so globalization will lead to stronger local cultures, not weaker ones.

Case study MTV Asia

In 1995, the cable television channel MTV introduced a new channel in Southeast Asia called MTV Asia. About one-fifth of the shows on MTV Asia come from the West, but the channel soon learned that viewers really wanted to hear local artists from Southeast Asia. MTV has now introduced other channels, focusing not just on regional, but also on national cultures, creating MTV Philippines, MTV Indonesia, and MTV Thailand.

MTV's cool new attitude toward local music, such as Dangdut music in Indonesia, has brought new life to some traditional musical styles, and made them popular around the world. However, it is clear from the MTV Asia charts that local artists do not rank highly in record sales—**Western** pop stars are more popular in Southeast Asia than ever before, and Western CDs are selling quickly to Asia's young people.

Globalization and You

People who feel strongly about globalization issues can express their opinions in various ways and make a difference. No one expects to change the world overnight, but working together with others to change one part of it can sometimes produce surprising results.

As a voter

People in **democratic** countries such as the United States and the United Kingdom can vote for politicians to represent them in government. Voters who have concerns about a particular issue can send a letter or e-mail to their local politician. They will often receive a detailed response. When voters express their views, it can affect how governments make decisions at international meetings.

As a campaigner

If it seems that a politician is not doing enough about an issue—or even if it seems that they are—it is possible to make a difference by joining a **campaign**. Some campaigners focus on changing the minds of politicians, to persuade them to change what the government does about the issue. This is called lobbying.

Other campaigners work directly to solve the issue without the government's help. This might involve asking people to change their habits as **consumers**, or approaching companies to ask them to change their behavior. It could include writing letters to newspapers or organizing an event.

As a consumer

Some people believe that consumers have the power to change how fair globalization will be. If consumers refuse to buy products that have been made unfairly, companies will make more of an effort to be fair in the future. If consumers buy only goods that have been made fairly, companies that produce goods fairly will benefit. For example, a brand of goods called Fairtrade is available in **Western** supermarkets. The brand promises to pay poor farmers in **developing countries** a fair price for their products. In some countries, sales of Fairtrade goods are growing by 100 percent each year, helping hundreds of thousands of developing country farmers out of poverty.

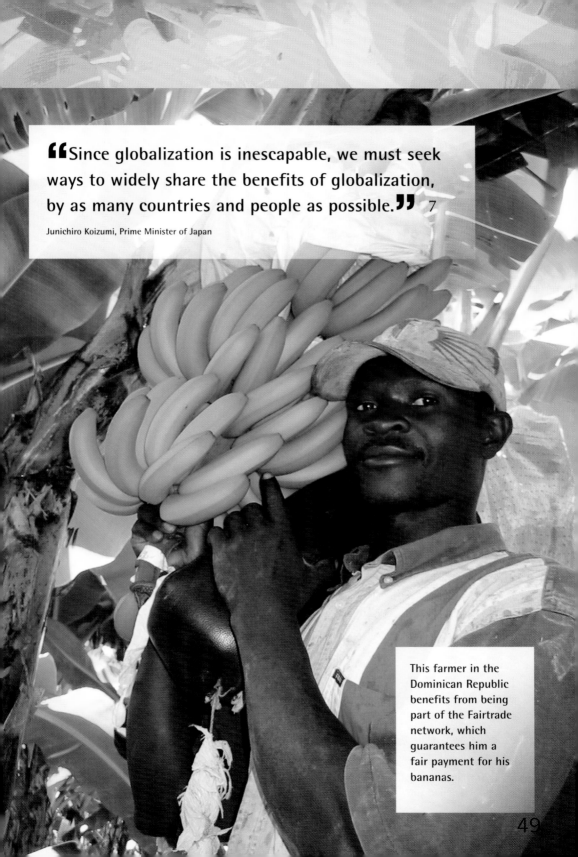

"Since globalization is inescapable, we must seek ways to widely share the benefits of globalization, by as many countries and people as possible." 7

Junichiro Koizumi, Prime Minister of Japan

This farmer in the Dominican Republic benefits from being part of the Fairtrade network, which guarantees him a fair payment for his bananas.

Facts and Figures

World exports

This is a record of the value of all the goods **traded** (bought and sold) between countries in the year stated.

Year	(Value in millions of dollars)
1950	295,621
1973	1,690,648
1990	3,456,762
2003	7,300,000

Source: The World Economy, Angus Maddison/OECD, IMF

World GDP

World GDP is a record of the value of the entire world's **economy**, including all business within all countries and all business between countries.

Year	(Value in millions of dollars)
1950	5,336,099
1973	16,059,177
1990	27,076,007
2003	36,356,240

Source: The World Economy, Angus Maddison/OECD, IMF

World exports as a percentage of world GDP

This is a record of how important trade between countries was in the given year, compared to, or as a percentage (%) of, the whole global economy (which also includes trade within countries).

Year	Percentage (%)
1950	5.5%
1973	10.5%
1990	12.8%
2003	20.0%

From the above two tables

Migration comparison

These statistics are estimates of the number of people who moved permanently from their country of origin to a new country.

Period	Total number (approximate figures)	As percentage (%) world population
1870–1910	155 million	10%
1975–2001	100 million	2%

Changed priorities of the World Bank (WB)

These figures show how spending decisions made by the **World Bank** changed between 1980 and 2002, switching from large projects such as providing power supplies towards social **services** such as healthcare.

Date	Percentage (%) of WB funds committed to developing power supplies	Percentage (%) of WB funds committed to developing social services
1980	21%	5%
2002	7%	22%

Development success in China

These statistics show the difference in growth between China's entire economy and its **import/export** businesses.

China:	Percentage (%) growth 1978–94
Entire economy	9% per year
Exports	14% per year
Imports	13% per year

Further Information

International organizations

The International Monetary Fund (IMF)
700 19th Street, NW
Washington, DC 20431
United States

The United Nations (UN)
First Avenue at 46th Street
New York, NY 10017
United States

The World Bank
1818 H Street, NW
Washington, DC 20433
United States

The World Trade Organization (WTO)
Centre William Rappard
Rue de Lausanne 154
CH-1211 Geneva 21
Switzerland

Campaigns

Amnesty International United States
322 Eighth Avenue
New York, NY 10001
Amnesty International campaigns to promote human rights.

Fairtrade
FLO International
Kaiser-Friedrich-Strasse 13
D-53113
Bonn
Germany

Jubilee USA Campaign
222 East Capitol Street, NE
Washington, DC 20003
The Jubilee campaign seeks an end to the debts poor countries have to pay to wealthy ones.

Further reading

Bowden, Rob, *21st Century Debates: Globalization*. (London: Hodder Wayland, 2003).

Connolly, Sean, *Citizen's Guide to the World Community*. (Oxford: Heinemann Library, 2002).

Morgan, Sally, *Science at the Edge: Global Warming*. (Oxford: Heinemann Library, 2002).

Reid, Struan, *Groundbreakers: Christopher Columbus*. (Oxford: Heinemann Library, 2003).

Teichmann, Iris, *In the News: Globalization*. (London: Franklin Watts, 2002).

Glossary

campaign
organized action to achieve a particular goal

capitalist
person or economy using capital (wealth) to profit from business activity

cargo
goods transported by ships, planes, or motor vehicles

communism
system of government in which the state controls the economy (an alternative to capitalism)

competition
rivalry between people or companies

consumer
person who is buying goods or a service

culture
ideas, arts, language, and behaviors of a society

currency
form of money of a particular country

debt payment
money paid back by a borrower to a lender

democracy
type of government in which leaders are chosen by voters

develop/development
move from poverty towards wealth; used especially when poor countries develop their industries and resources

developed country
wealthy country that is economically advanced

developing country
poor or non-industrial country that is trying to develop its resources

economic growth
increasing a country's wealth and raising its living standards

economy
wealth and resources of a country or region

empire
group of countries ruled by a single country or person

exports
goods that are sold and sent to another country

free trade
buying and selling goods without limits or rules

global warming
gradual increase in the overall temperature worldwide, believed to be caused by the greenhouse effect

grant
sum of money distributed for a specific purpose, for example by a government, with no repayment required

human rights
rights belonging to all individuals

immigrant
person who moves to live permanently in another country

imports
goods or services brought into a country from abroad

Industrial Revolution
period in the 18th and 19th centuries in which Western industries grew rapidly

inflation
rise in prices and fall in the purchasing power of money

interest
payment made to a lender in exchange for the temporary use of their money

interest-free credit
money lent to a borrower that requires no interest to be paid

International Monetary Fund (IMF)
international organization that helps to keep currencies stable and lends large sums of money to countries in times of crisis

invest
use money to buy something with the goal of making a profit

malnutrition
unhealthiness caused by poor diet or starvation

migration
movement from one area or country to another

pesticide
chemical used to fight insects that attack crops or farm animals

politics
beliefs and actions to do with running society

profit
money gained by an individual or business after selling something for more than it cost to buy or produce

refugee
person fleeing a natural or social disaster in their home country

service
something, other than goods, that is provided for money (such as entertainment)

society
country, community, or group of people, organized according to certain rules

subsidy
sum of money given to help a particular type of business make a profit

tariff
special tax designed to restrict a particular type of import

trade
act of buying and selling goods and services, especially between nations

United Nations (UN)
international organization set up to promote international peace, cooperation, and security

USSR
Union of Soviet Socialist Republics, the large communist state (country) that existed in and around Russia from 1922–91

Western
countries that share common roots in European social, cultural, and economic activities

World Bank
international banking organization that lends money to developing countries

World Trade Organization (WTO)
international organization that tries to promote free trade and economic development

Index